Spot the Differences

Butterfly or Moth?

by Adeline J. Zimmerman

Bullfrog
Books

Ideas for Parents and Teachers

Bullfrog Books let children practice reading informational text at the earliest reading levels. Repetition, familiar words, and photo labels support early readers.

Before Reading

• Discuss the cover photo. What does it tell them?

• Look at the picture glossary together. Read and discuss the words.

Read the Book

• "Walk" through the book and look at the photos. Let the child ask questions. Point out the photo labels.

• Read the book to the child, or have him or her read independently.

After Reading

• Prompt the child to think more. Ask: Have you ever seen a butterfly or moth? If so, where was the insect? What was it doing?

Bullfrog Books are published by Jump!
5357 Penn Avenue South
Minneapolis, MN 55419
www.jumplibrary.com

Library of Congress Cataloging-in-Publication Data

Names: Zimmerman, Adeline J., author.
Title: Butterfly or moth? / by Adeline J. Zimmerman.
Description: Bullfrog books. Minneapolis, MN: Jump!, Inc., [2022]
Series: Spot the differences
Includes index. | Audience: Ages 5–8
Identifiers: LCCN 2021028389 (print)
LCCN 2021028390 (ebook)
ISBN 9781636903408 (hardcover)
ISBN 9781636903415 (paperback)
ISBN 9781636903422 (ebook)
Subjects: LCSH: Butterflies—Juvenile literature.
Moths—Juvenile literature.
Classification: LCC QL544.2 .Z56 2022 (print)
LCC QL544.2 (ebook)
DDC 595.78/9—dc23
LC record available at https://lccn.loc.gov/2021028389
LC ebook record available at https://lccn.loc.gov/2021028390

Editor: Jenna Gleisner
Designer: Michelle Sonnek

Photo Credits: Sari ONeal/Shutterstock, cover (left); xpixel/Shutterstock, cover (right); Matee Nuserm/Shutterstock, 1 (left), 24 (top); Cosmin Manci/Shutterstock, 1 (right); James Laurie/Shutterstock, 3, 10–11; deborah kania/iStock, 4; Jussi Lindberg/Shutterstock, 5, 14–15; Huaykwang/Shutterstock, 6–7 (top); Independent birds/Shutterstock, 6–7 (bottom); Cathy Keifer/Shutterstock, 8–9, 23tr, 23br; Lukas Gojda/Shutterstock, 12–13; SAND555/iStock, 16–17; Jim and Lynne Weber/Shutterstock, 18–19; BOONCHUAY PROMJIAM/Shutterstock, 20, 23tl, 23bl; heibaihui/iStock, 21; Shutterstock, 22; Melinda Fawver/Shutterstock, 24 (bottom).

Printed in the United States of America at Corporate Graphics in North Mankato, Minnesota.

Table of Contents

A moth is fuzzy.
A butterfly is smooth.
Which is this?

How to Use This Book

In this book, you will see pictures of both butterflies and moths. Can you tell which one is in each picture?

Hint: You can find the answers if you flip the book upside down!

See Them Fly!

This is a butterfly.

This is a moth.

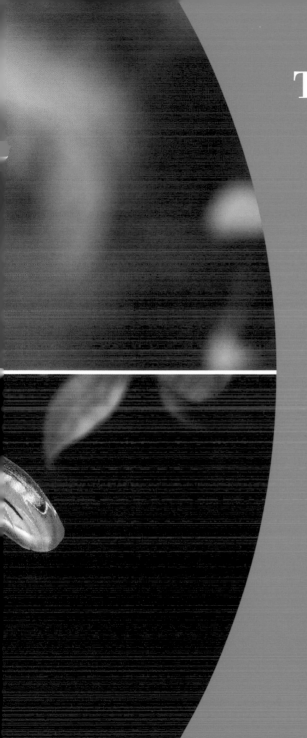

They look the same.
But they are not.
How?

Let's see!

Both have antennas.
A butterfly's are thin.
A moth's are thick.
They look like combs.
Which is this?

Answer: moth

antenna

A moth is fuzzy.

A butterfly is smooth.

Which is this?

Both have big wings.

A butterfly has bright wings.

It stands out.

Which is this?

wing

A moth has dull wings.
It hides.
Which is this?

Answer: moth

Both fly.

A moth flies at night.

A butterfly flies
in the day.

Which is this?

Both rest.

A moth's wings lie down.

A butterfly's fold up.

Which is this?

Good night!

See and Compare

long, thin antennas

bright wings

long, smooth body

Moth

wide, comb-like antennas

dull wings

short, fuzzy body

Quick Facts

Butterflies and moths are both insects. They both have wings and antennas. They are similar, but they have differences. Take a look!

Butterflies

- are diurnal, meaning they are most active and fly during the day

- have bright wings to scare predators

- start out as caterpillars and make chrysalises to grow in

Moths

- are nocturnal, meaning they are most active and fly at night

- have dull wings to blend in and hide from predators

- start out as a fuzzy caterpillars and make cocoons to grow in

Picture Glossary

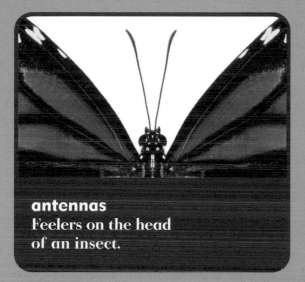

antennas
Feelers on the head
of an insect.

fuzzy
Covered in short, soft hairs.

smooth
Having an even surface
without roughness or bumps.

thick
Great in width or depth.
Not thin.

Index

To Learn More

Finding more information is as easy as 1, 2, 3.

① Go to www.factsurfer.com

② Enter "butterflyormoth?" into the search box.

③ Choose your book to see a list of websites.